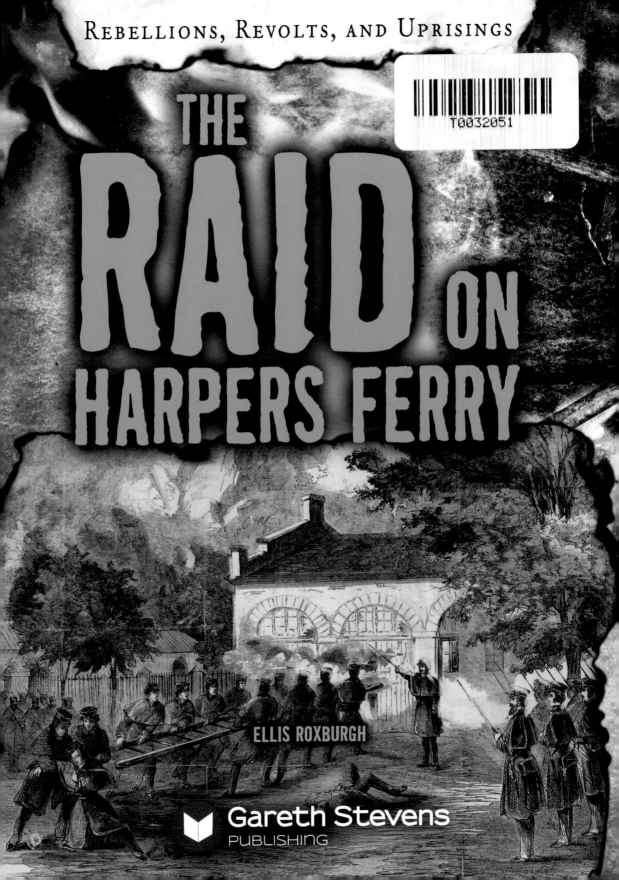

THE RAID ON HARPERS FERRY

ELLIS ROXBURGH

Gareth Stevens
PUBLISHING

T0032051

Please visit our website, www.garethstevens.com. For a free color catalog of all our high-quality books, call toll-free 1-800-542-2595 or fax 1-877-542-2596.

CATALOGING-IN-PUBLICATION DATA

Names: Roxburgh, Ellis.
Title: The raid on Harpers Ferry / Ellis Roxburgh.
Description: New York : Gareth Stevens Publishing, 2018. | Series: Rebellions, revolts, and uprisings | Includes index.
Identifiers: ISBN 9781538207741 (pbk.) | ISBN 9781538207666 (library bound) | ISBN 9781538207543 (6 pack)
Subjects: LCSH: Brown, John, 1800-1859--Juvenile literature. | Antislavery movements--United States--History--
    19th century--Juvenile literature. | Harpers Ferry (W. Va.)--History--John Brown's Raid, 1859--
    Juvenile literature.
Classification: LCC E451.R69 2018 | DDC 973.7'116--dc23

Published in 2018 by
Gareth Stevens Publishing
111 East 14th Street, Suite 349
New York, NY 10003

For Brown Bear Books Ltd:
Managing Editor: Tim Cooke
Designer: Lynne Lennon
Editorial Director: Lindsey Lowe
Children's Publisher: Anne O'Daly
Design Manager: Keith Davis
Picture Manager: Sophie Mortimer

Picture Credits
Cover: Getty: Interim Archive, Archive Photos Collection
Interior: Alamy: North Wind Picture Archives 17; Library of Congress: 8, 9, 10, 11, 18, 19, 20, 23, 25, 28, 29, 30, 33, 38, 39, 41, 42, 43; NARA: 31, 35; Public Domain: Acroterion 22, 36, MamaGeek 26, National Portrait Gallery, Smithsonian Institute 12, Smallbones 21; Shutterstock: Dave Allen Photography 15, Everett Historical 4, 6, 7, 13, 14, 16, 27, 32, 34, 37, 40; Thinkstock: istockphoto 5, 24.

All other images Brown Bear Books

Brown Bear Books has made every attempt to contact the copyright holder.
If anyone has any information please contact licensing@brownbearbooks.co.uk

Manufactured in the United States of America

CPSIA compliance information: Batch #CS17GS. For further information contact Gareth Stevens, New York, New York at 1-800-542-2595.

CONTENTS

WORDS IN THE GLOSSARY APPEAR IN **BOLD** TYPE
THE FIRST TIME THEY ARE USED IN THE TEXT.

ROOTS OF REBELLION

The roots of the 1859 raid on Harpers Ferry by John Brown lay in 2 centuries of African American slavery. Brown spent his life fighting something he thought was unchristian and wrong.

Slavery had existed in America since the early 1600s. Africans were taken from their homeland and shipped across the Atlantic Ocean. They were sold into slavery in America. There, they had no rights. Slaves became the property of their owners.

←

African slaves are sold at an auction in the United States.

From the start of the 1800s, industrialization began to transform the northern states. White European immigrants arrived in the United States in large numbers. There was no longer a need for African American slaves in the North. Meanwhile, however, in the South the invention of the **cotton gin** had dramatically increased the demand for cotton. Cotton was a **labor-intensive** crop and plantation owners needed more slaves to work in the fields. The price of slaves increased steadily from 1814. Southerners called slavery a "peculiar **institution**." They believed Northerners could not understand it. The issue of slavery was increasingly dividing the country.

The cotton gin enabled cotton to be processed more quickly and cheaply than before.

THE 1820 MISSOURI COMPROMISE

UNDER THE TERMS OF THE MISSOURI **COMPROMISE**, MISSOURI WAS ALLOWED TO ENTER THE UNION AS A SLAVE STATE. IN RETURN, A NEW FREE STATE NAMED MAINE WAS CREATED FROM PART OF MASSACHUSETTS. THIS PRESERVED THE NUMERICAL BALANCE IN CONGRESS. IN ADDITION, THE ACT ADDED THAT SLAVERY WOULD NOT BE ALLOWED TO EXIST IN ANY NEW STATES NORTH OF A LATITUDE OF 36°30' NORTH, WHICH WAS MISSOURI'S SOUTHERN BORDER.

A Nation Divided

Until 1820, the United States had an equal number of slave states (those that permitted slavery) and free states (those that didn't permit slavery). Missouri asked to join the country as a slave state. If it joined, the balance of power in government would be tilted toward slave states.

During the early 1800s, Americans were starting to head west to settle. By 1849, thousands headed even further to California where gold had been found.

Fugitive slaves flee from Maryland to find freedom in the North.

In order to keep the balance, politicians came up with the Missouri Compromise. This created the new state of Maine from the state of Massachusetts. Maine was a free state where slavery was banned. This meant that there were now 11 slave-holding states and 11 where slavery was banned.

The fragile compromise did not last long. The country was expanding rapidly westward. The question soon arose about whether new states created in the West would permit slavery or not. In the 1850s, the question of slavery came to a head in the Kansas Territory.

This map of 1856 uses dark gray to indicate the slave states. ↑

The Balance Changes Again

As settlers moved into Kansas in the 1850s, there were violent clashes between those who wanted the territory to become a free state and those who wanted it to become a slave state.

In 1849, the gold rush drew settlers to the West Coast. California's population grew and it joined the Union as a free state in 1850. The balance between slave and non-slave states was now uneven. To keep the Southern states happy, a new compromise was signed in 1850. The compromise included the **Fugitive** Slave Act. The act laid out harsh punishments for anyone who did not help recapture runaway slaves. In the North, many people were outraged. They defied the law by trying to help escaped slaves who had reached the North.

"Bleeding Kansas"

In 1854, the Kansas–Nebraska Act gave residents of these two new territories the right to decide whether to join the Union as slave or free states. Few people then lived in Nebraska, but in Kansas, **skirmishes** broke out between supporters and opponents of slavery. Kansas became known as "bleeding Kansas" because of the bloodshed. Opposing groups of **activists** from the North and the South moved to Kansas to try to influence the state's decision.

This political cartoon of the time shows Liberty trying to stop the violence in Kansas.

LIBERTY. THE FAIR MAID OF KANSAS_IN THE HANDS OF THE "BORDER RUFFIANS"

9

FRANK LESLIE'S
ILLUSTRATED
NEWS PAPER

No. 92.—VOL. IV.] NEW YORK, SATURDAY, JUNE 27, 1857. [PRICE 6 CENTS.

This newspaper report describes the Dred Scott trial.

The Dred Scott Case

In March 1857, the US Supreme Court issued an influential decision. A slave named Dred Scott asked to be declared a free man because he had lived in a free state with his master. The Supreme Court turned down Scott's request. It judged that slave owners could take their slaves into free states without fear of losing them. Again, the ruling outraged opponents of slavery in the North. Increasingly, **abolitionists** began to call for the ending of slavery all throughout the United States.

America Before Harpers Ferry

In 1857 changes in European trade caused an economic **depression** in the United States. The effects were felt particularly in the South. Exports of tobacco and cotton fell. Meanwhile, in the North, large numbers of immigrants from Europe worked in factories and sweatshops in New York City and other industrial cities. Slavery was forbidden in the North, but African Americans were not treated equally.

Abraham Lincoln

While he was trying to become the Republican presidential candidate, Abraham Lincoln gave a speech in February 1860 after the raid on Harpers Ferry. Lincoln condemned the leader of the raid, John Brown, as a violent fanatic. However, Lincoln argued that the abolitionist north must also align with the West, which was mainly free, to get rid of slavery. Lincoln won the Republican candidacy in May 1860 and was elected president in November of that year.

Abraham Lincoln was a lawyer from Illinois.

Presidential Election

A presidential election was due in 1860. This made Southerners anxious. A new political party, the Republican Party, had been created in 1854 to oppose slavery. Slaveholders were concerned that the party would propose an abolitionist as their presidential candidate. Their fears were realized. The Republican candidate was an opponent of slavery named Abraham Lincoln. However, the question of whether to abolish slavery was not part of the presidential campaign.

WHO WERE THE REBELS?

During the bitter struggles over slavery in Kansas, a man named John Brown decided that it was time to take a stand for freedom.

John Brown was born in Torrington, Connecticut, on May 9, 1800. When he was 5 years old, his family moved west to Ohio, which then lay on the western frontier of the United States. In Ohio, the Brown family became friendly with many of the Native Americans and freed slaves who lived there. John's mother died when he was just 8 years old. He felt her loss for the rest of his life.

←

This photograph shows John Brown in 1846, at around the time he began planning to free the slaves.

John Brown's Letter

THE REASON WE KNOW SO MUCH ABOUT THE YOUNG JOHN BROWN IS BECAUSE OF A LETTER HE WROTE. IN 1857, A 10-YEAR-OLD BOY IN BOSTON WROTE BROWN TO ASK HIM WHAT KIND OF BOY HE HAD BEEN. BROWN'S LONG REPLY DESCRIBES HIS EARLY LIFE. IT ALSO EXPLAINS THE INCIDENTS THAT STIRRED HIS VIOLENT OPPOSITION TO SLAVERY.

Sympathy for Slaves

The Brown family had a strong sense of social justice. When he was aged 12, John helped his father drive cattle for sale to a US Army barracks at Fort Detroit. On the way, they stayed with a friend who owned a young slave boy, with whom John became friendly. John saw how badly dressed the slave boy was and how differently he was treated from free children. He felt sorry for this vulnerable young child.

→

As a child, Brown was struck by the terrible conditions in which slave children his age were forced to live.

13

SLAVE REBELLIONS

JOHN BROWN WAS NOT THE FIRST PERSON TO BELIEVE THAT SLAVERY IN THE UNITED STATES COULD BE DESTROYED BY AN UPRISING OF SLAVES. IN 1800, TWO SLAVE BROTHERS, GABRIEL AND MARTIN PROSSER, HAD PLANNED TO RISE UP AGAINST WHITES IN RICHMOND, VIRGINIA. THE BROTHERS WERE BETRAYED BY OTHER SLAVES AND ARRESTED AND HANGED BEFORE THEIR REVOLT COULD BEGIN. IN 1831, A SLAVE NAMED NAT TURNER LED A SLAVE REBELLION IN SOUTHAMPTON COUNTY, VIRGINIA. HE AND HIS ACCOMPLICES KILLED AROUND 60 WHITES BEFORE THEY WERE CAPTURED AND EXECUTED. THERE HAD BEEN OTHER MINOR SLAVE RISINGS, TOO—BUT NONE HAD EVER SUCCEEDED.

Later Life

John Brown married twice. He fathered 20 children although many of them died while they were still infants. After the death in 1832 of his first wife, Dianthe, Brown tried to make money by buying frontier land. At the time, land **speculation** was very popular.

Mrs. John Brown & two of her children, from daguerreotype –

← John Brown married Mary Ann in 1833. She is shown here with two of their children.

But in 1837, economic changes in Europe and a collapse in land prices in the American West led to one of the biggest financial crashes in US history. Brown lost all his money. Like many other Americans he was left in debt. He had a new wife, Mary Ann, and his children to support.

The Plan

Sometime in the mid-1840s, while Brown was still struggling to feed his family, he began thinking about ways to end slavery. Brown planned to recruit up to 100 freedom fighters. They would base themselves in the Blue Ridge Mountains, where they would hide from the **authorities**.

Brown hoped to be able to hide out in the Blue Ridge Mountains.

ABOLITIONIST LEADER

FREDERICK DOUGLASS (C.1818-1895) WAS BORN A SLAVE IN MARYLAND. HE ESCAPED TO MASSACHUSETTS WHEN HE WAS AGED 20. HE WORKED AS A LABORER UNTIL HE BECAME A SPOKESMAN FOR THE GROWING ABOLITIONIST MOVEMENT. WITH HIS DISTINGUISHED APPEARANCE AND HIS SKILL AT PUBLIC SPEAKING, PEOPLE FOUND IT HARD TO BELIEVE HE HAD BEEN A SLAVE.

Douglass was a friend of Brown but opposed his methods.
←

Brown planned to use the Blue Ridge Mountains as a base to raid slaveholding communities in Virginia and Maryland. He hoped that if he carried out repeated attacks he could frighten the slaveholders and they would become **disillusioned**. In the end, he thought they would abandon slavery. He also thought that the slaves would escape as soon as they had the chance.

Brown discussed his plans with friends he hoped would join him. One of the first people he told was the former slave Frederick Douglass. The two men met in 1847. Douglass had become a prominent leader of the abolitionist campaign.

↑ Pro- and antislavery supporters fight in Fort Scott, Kansas.

Words of Warning

John Brown and Frederick Douglass remained friends for over a decade, but they did not agree about the best way to achieve the abolition of slavery. Although Douglass appreciated the strength of Brown's dedication to the abolition movement, he was against his plan to recruit freedom fighters. Douglass believed that persuading the slaveholders to give up their slaves had more chance of success than turning toward violence. He also warned Brown that he might lose his life while he was fighting for the cause. Brown replied that such a **sacrifice** would be worth it.

Fugitive Slave Act

The Fugitive Slave Act of 1850 was passed as part of the compromise between slave and free states. It forced everyone to help return escaped slaves to their owners, even from free states in the North. Abolitionists called the act the "Bloodhound Law" because slavers used dogs to track down runaway slaves. They argued that the act forced them to support slavery even if they were against it. They also argued that it allowed even free blacks in the North to be harassed.

White men capture African Americans they believe to be escaped slaves in this illustration from the time.

"Old Brown"

In October 1855, John Brown moved his family to Kansas. He organized a **militia** group of "Free Staters" who opposed slavery. Brown wanted to fight the proslavery groups active in Kansas. Brown's militia skirmished with the "Border Ruffians." These proslavers crossed into Kansas from neighboring Missouri to try to **terrorize** Kansans into accepting slavery.

On May 21, 1856, Brown and his men looked on as Border Ruffians attacked and burned the town of Lawrence, which was home to many opponents of slavery. Then news came of a near-fatal attack in the US Senate on a leading antislavery senator, Charles Sumner of Massachusetts.

Brown was determined to get revenge for these attacks. On May 24, 1856, he led his men in an attack on the proslavery Doyle family in their cabin on Pottawatomie Creek. Brown's men killed five men in what became known as the Pottawatomie **Massacre**. Brown defended his attack by claiming that it was repayment for the burning of Lawrence and the attack on Sumner. In return, Border Ruffians destroyed Brown's home, killing a number of his followers.

The Secret Six

Brown went on the run. People now saw him as a dangerous extremist. However, he made his way to the North. There, abolitionists in the North were growing more determined to end slavery. Brown met leading abolitionists in Massachusetts who agreed to support his cause by supplying money and weapons. They became known as the "Secret Six."

The raid on Lawrence, Kansas, was one incident that led to Brown's decision to act.

REBELLION!

By the time John Brown was ready to attack Harpers Ferry in October 1859, he had been thinking about how to end slavery for more than a decade.

Harpers Ferry lies in the shadow of the Blue Ridge Mountains on two rivers, the Shenandoah and the Potomac. The town is now in West Virginia, but in the mid-1800s it was part of Virginia. In 1799, the town was selected as the site of one of two national **armories**. The armory manfactured and stored small arms for the US Army. It was created so that the **federal** government did not have to rely on private arms manufacturers. The town was selected for the armory because of its transportation links. In addition to the two rivers, the town stood on the junction of two railroads.

→ Harpers Ferry was home to numerous buildings of the US Armory.

A Federal Target

Brown did not target Harpers Ferry because he wanted to steal arms. He already had enough weapons for his own men. Abolitionists in the North had secretly sent him 200 rifles to be used in the planned attack.

In part, Brown chose the town because he knew news of an attack on a federal armory would soon spread. He believed that local slaves who heard the news would be eager to join him. His intention was to steal weapons from the arsenal to arm these additional slaves rushing to join his uprising.

Brown stayed at this house in Chambersburg, Pennsylvania, as he made his early plans for the raid.

The raiders rented the Kennedy Farmhouse outside Harpers Ferry.

Brown and his men rented a farmhouse just north of Harpers Ferry. They stayed there for 3 months as Brown visited the town and planned the raid. Brown decided to attack three parts of the US armory. The most important target was the **musket** factory. It was thought to hold 100,000 muskets. Muskets were the standard weapons of the day, so they would be most useful in the uprising.

Attack!

At sundown on October 16, 1859, John Brown, two of his sons, and 18 other men left the Kennedy farmhouse. They set out on foot for Harpers Ferry, 4 miles (6.4 km) away. More men would follow them later. The attackers included five African Americans, but the number was far below the hundred freedom fighters Brown had been hoping to attract.

The raiders walked all night in heavy rain. As they crossed the Potomac River, they cut the **telegraph** wires to the town. Brown figured that would give them 24 hours before word of the raid spread.

Brown's men reached Harpers Ferry at 4 a.m. Their first target was the federal **arsenal**. It was only defended by one guard, so they captured it easily. Brown then sent five of his men to capture Colonel Lewis Washington.

Washington was one of the leading citizens of the town. He was a relative of George Washington and was also a slaveholder. Brown had decided that the colonel would be an ideal **hostage**. So far, things were going well.

→

John Brown had met Colonel Lewis Washington when he visited Harpers Ferry to plan the raid.

23

The Telegraph

The invention of the telegraph in the 1830s and 1840s by Samuel Morse revolutionized long-distance communications in America. The telegraph sent electrical signals over a wire to carry messages. It played a key role in the raid on Harpers Ferry. The president was alerted to the attack and sent troops to join the Virginia militia who had also learned of the attack via the telegraph.

Telegraph operators used a key to tap out messages in long and short strokes.

Plans Go Wrong

Brown's plans soon began to go wrong, however. His men stopped the Ohio–Baltimore train as it passed through Harpers Ferry. In the confusion, the train's night porter, a free black man, was shot dead.

When Brown found out what had happened, he ordered that the train be allowed to leave. This proved to be a mistake. At the next town, the conductor sent a telegram warning of the attack. The news reached Washington, DC, at around 11 a.m. on October 17, 1859.

Meanwhile, Brown waited for the slave uprising he had expected. It did not happen. Around 40 slaves helped the attackers, but it is not known whether they joined willingly or through force. Certainly, this was far from the hundreds or thousands of slaves that Brown had anticipated. It seemed that the slaves were not waiting for the chance to revolt, after all.

It proved to be a mistake to allow the Ohio–Baltimore train to leave Harpers Ferry.

An Eyewitness Account

One of the reasons that we know so much about the planning and the events of Harpers Ferry is because Osborne Anderson survived the raid and wrote an account of the events. *A Voice from Harpers Ferry* was published in 1861. Osborne Anderson was an African American and he went on to serve in the Union Army in the Civil War (1861–1865).

↑ Brown's men were based in the Engine House, where fire engines were kept.

John Brown had also mistaken the reaction of local people in Harpers Ferry and its neighbor, Charles Town. He had imagined that they would be terrified and would be happy to help the raiders. Instead, the townspeople offered no support. Brown managed to persuade the owner of the town hotel, the Wager House Hotel, to provide breakfast for his men and their hostages, but that was the only support he and his men received from the townspeople.

Before long, Brown began to argue with his men. Having failed to start a slave uprising, some were now fearing reaction to the raid. They wanted to leave Harpers Ferry at once and escape to safety.

Brown himself seemed to be confused. He could not understand why slaves from the area were not flocking to the town to join the **insurrection**. One of his followers, an African American named Osborne Anderson, later noted that, "Captain Brown was all activity, though I could not help thinking that at times he appeared somewhat puzzled."

In this illustration, a slave owner talks to slaves who did not join Brown's raid.

FIGHTING AUTHORITY

The US government was quick to respond to Brown's attack. Fearing the worst, President James Buchanan sent his best men to Harpers Ferry.

News of the raid on Harpers Ferry reached Washington, DC, in the middle of the morning on October 17, 1859. Buchanan at once met with his secretary of war, John Floyd. The men were both shocked. They had not expected an attack of this sort. They were worried that the attack would spread to the capital. Many slaves worked in homes in Washington. It would be serious if they joined an uprising.

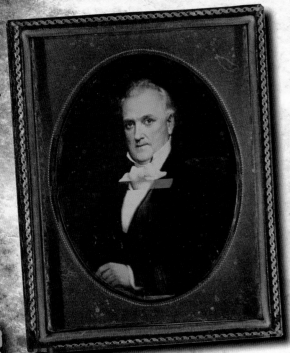

← *James Buchanan was US president from 1857 to 1861.*

Militia and cizitens head for Harpers Ferry after news of the raid spread.

Floyd ordered the US Marine base in Annapolis to prepare to deal with the uprising. Floyd requested that Lieutenant Colonel Robert E. Lee lead the Marines, accompanied by Lieutenant J.E.B. Stuart. Still dressed in their civilian clothes, Lee and Stuart set off immediately for Washington, DC, to receive their orders.

An Armed Response

Meanwhile, as soon as news of the attack spread in Virginia, militia groups started to assemble. Just before noon on October 17, Brown heard footsteps on the Potomac Bridge. He imagined they came from escaping slaves.

OUTSTANDING COMMANDER

ROBERT E. LEE WAS ONE OF THE OUTSTANDING MILITARY COMMANDERS OF HIS GENERATION. HE GRADUATED TOP IN HIS CLASS AT THE US MILITARY ACADEMY AT WEST POINT. AFTER SERVING IN THE US ARMY, HE SIDED WITH THE CONFEDERATES IN THE CIVIL WAR. HE COMMANDED THE ARMY OF NORTHERN VIRGINIA FROM 1862 UNTIL THE CONFEDERACY FELL. LEE SURRENDERED THE CONFEDERATE ARMY AT APPOMATTOX COURT HOUSE ON APRIL 9, 1865.

In fact, the footsteps Brown heard belonged to the Virginia militia. Brown's men fired at the new arrivals, who temporarily fell back. Before long, however, the militia had the raiders boxed into a small area of the town.

In the gun battle that followed, the raiders proved better shots than the militia. However, as more militiamen were shot, the citizens who had gathered to watch grew angry with the raiders. Brown then made another mistake.

← The Virginia militia had a long record of military service.

Robert E. Lee wrote to Brown
demanding his surrender.

Brown divided his fighters. While the main group took
shelter in the brick fire engine house, he sent a smaller group
to the rifle works 300 yards (275 m) away. The militia soon
overpowered the small group and killed their leader.

A Truce?

Brown was starting to realize that his rebellion had failed.
He had lost four men. He was trapped in the engine house
with gunfire all around. No slaves had joined the uprising—
and now the militia would stop them even if they tried.

But Brown still believed he could get out of his situation. He decided to send two of his men out with a white flag of **truce**. He wanted to make a deal. In return for being allowed to cross the river to Maryland, he would release his hostages. But the crowd gathered outside was becoming rowdy. When the two messengers emerged, their flag was shot to pieces. They beat a retreat back inside the engine house.

The Tipping Point

As the afternoon wore on, the townsfolk gathered in the Wager House Hotel became drunk. Then one of the rebels in the engine house shot and killed the town's mayor, Fontaine Beckham. The townspeople and the militia were

The two sides fire at each other in the battle at the engine house.

CAVALRY LEADER

JEB STUART WAS A US MARINE OFFICER WHO LATER JOINED THE CONFEDERATE ARMY DURING THE CIVIL WAR. HE WAS A HIGHLY SKILLED CAVALRY COMMANDER. HE ALSO ACTED AS ROBERT E. LEE'S EYES AND EARS AMONG HIS FELLOW SOLDIERS, WITH WHOM HE WAS VERY POPULAR. HE WAS SHOT BY A UNION SOLDIER AND DIED ON MAY 12, 1864.

J.E.B. Stuart was known as Jeb, from his initials.

enraged. When three of Brown's men tried to escape, the militia killed two of them. The bodies of the dead **insurgents** were left where they fell.

The situation was desperate. John Brown clung to the hope that hundreds of slaves might still show up to support him. Instead, Colonel Lee and 120 marines arrived at around 11 p.m. on October 17.

DID YOU KNOW?
ROBERT E. LEE LATER DESCRIBED BROWN'S PLAN FOR THE RAID ON HARPERS FERRY AS "THE ATTEMPT OF A FANATIC OR MADMAN."

The Last Day

By the morning, Brown had only three men left alive. His son, Oliver, had been wounded the previous day and had died in the night. J.E.B. Stuart approached the engine house and handed Brown a letter demanding a full surrender. Brown refused. He still wanted to leave across the Potomac River.

Lee gave the order to storm the engine house. A dozen marines broke down the door, one of whom was shot dead. In the short fight that followed, Brown and another rebel, Aaron Stevens, were badly wounded with swords. The last two raiders were killed. The uprising was over.

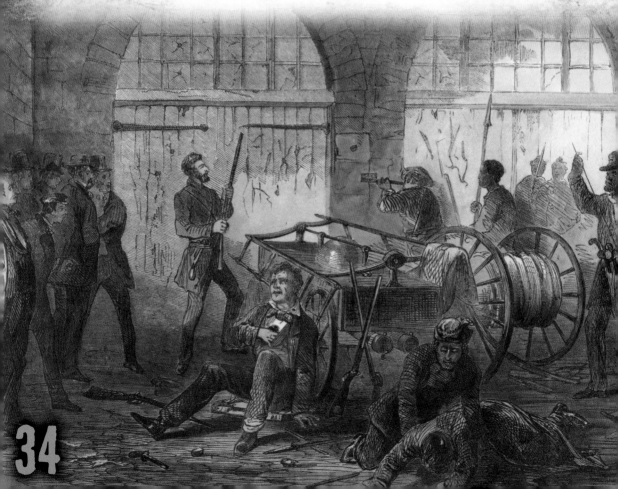

↓ *John Brown lies wounded at the end of the fight for the engine house.*

HARPERS FERRY OCT.XIXTH. HON.SECY OF WAR. WASHN. . I FIND A PERFECT

PANIC HERE. YOU MUST BY ALL MEANS DETAIL A TROOP TO MY RELIEF

IMMEDIATELY. THE MARINES WILL LEAVE. A.M.BARBOUR. SUPT.U.S.ARMORY

The superintendent of the Armory sent a telegram asking for reinforcements.

The Aftermath

Of the original party of raiders and some later arrivals, 10 had been killed and seven more captured. Five had managed to escape. Brown and Stevens were still in danger of dying from their wounds. They were laid out on the grass in front of the engine house, where Lee protected them from the angry militia to make sure they were not **lynched**.

Brown and Stevens were taken to the paymaster's office for questioning. The governor of Virginia, Henry Wise, arrived to help with the **interrogation**. The interrogation lasted 3 hours. Despite being weak from his wounds, Brown told Wise exactly what he had done and why.

DID YOU KNOW?
JOHN BROWN WAS DEEPLY CUT ON THE BACK OF HIS NECK BY A BLOW FROM A SABRE, A TYPE OF SHARP, CURVING SWORD. THE WOUND NEARLY KILLED HIM.

35

DEFEAT AND LEGACY

John Brown's trial divided the United States. To many Northerners he was a martyr, but most Southerners saw him as a terrorist.

Brown was sent for trial in Charles Town, Virginia, on October 25, 1859. Still suffering from his wounds, he could barely walk into the courtroom. Once in place, he had to lie on a mattress. He spent most of the 5 days of the trial lying on the floor. By the time the trial began, Brown had become the most famous man in America.

The trial took place in Charles Town, next to Harpers Ferry.

Brown on his mattress (front) during his trial. ↑

Brown's actions divided the country. For those who opposed slavery, he was a hero. He might be a badly flawed hero, because he had used violence, but at least his intentions were honorable. To supporters of slavery, meanwhile, he was a figure of hatred whom they thought deserved to die.

Brown's lawyer urged him to plead insanity. There was a history of insanity in the Brown family, so Brown could argue that he had not been in his right mind. Brown refused.

The Verdict

Brown was on trial with his fellow captives, but in reality the trial was focused entirely on him. He spent the time napping on his mattress and seemed unconcerned about proceedings.

Brown's only concern was to insist that he had not hurt any peaceful observer during the raid. On November 1, 1859, the jury retired to consider its verdict. Forty-five minutes later they returned. They found Brown guilty. He was then allowed to sit up and address the court. Brown made a powerful speech in which he said that it was his defense of the powerless that had led to his guilty verdict.

Death Sentence

Brown and the other raiders were sentenced to hang. During the weeks before his execution, Brown lived in the Charles Town jail. He received visits from many supporters. People wrote to him from across the country, praising his sacrifice for the abolitionist cause.

Thanks to Brown's raid, the question of whether slavery should be allowed was being debated in American homes.

→

This illustration shows Brown delivering his speech in court.

Brown's Address to the Court

"Had I interfered ... in behalf of the rich, the powerful, the intelligent, the so-called great, or in behalf of any of their friends ... and suffered and sacrificed what I have in this interference, it would have been all right; and every man in this court would have deemed it an act worthy of reward rather than punishment."

→

Brown's address to the court was widely reported and admired.

ADDRESS OF JOHN BROWN

To the Virginia Court, when about to receive the

SENTENCE OF DEATH,

For his heroic attempt at Harper's Ferry, to

Give deliverance to the captives, and to let the oppressed go free.

[Mr. Brown, upon inquiry whether he had anything to say why sentence should not be pronounced upon him, in a clear, distinct voice, replied :]

I have, may it please the Court, a few words to say.

In the first place, I deny every thing but what I have already admitted, of a design on my part to *free Slaves*. I intended, certainly, to have made a clean thing of that matter, as I did last winter, when I went into Missouri, and there took Slaves, without the snapping of a gun on either side, moving them through the country, and finally leaving them in Canada. I desired to have done the same thing again, on a much larger scale. *That was all I intended.* I never did intend murder, or treason, or the destruction of property, or to excite or incite Slaves to rebellion, or to make insurrection.

I have another objection, and that is, that it is *unjust* that I should suffer such a penalty. Had I interfered in the manner, and which I admit has been fairly proved,—for I admire the truthfulness and candor of the greater portion of the witnesses who have testified in this case,—had I so interfered in behalf of the Rich, the Powerful, the Intelligent, the so-called Great, or in behalf of any of their friends, either father, mother, brother, sister, wife, or children, or any of *that class*, and suffered and sacrificed what I have in this interference, *it would have been all right.* Every man in this Court would have deemed it an act worthy a reward, rather than a punishment.

This Court acknowledges too, as I suppose, the validity of the LAW OF GOD. I saw a book kissed, which I suppose to be the BIBLE, or at least the NEW TESTAMENT, which teaches me that, "All things whatsoever I would that men should do to me, I should do even so to them." It teaches me further, to "Remember them that are in bonds, as bound with them." I endeavored to act up to that instruction.

I say I am yet too young to understand that GOD is any *respecter of persons.* I believe that to have interfered as I have done, as I have always freely admitted I have done, in behalf of his *despised poor,* I have done no wrong, but RIGHT.

Now, if it is deemed necessary that I should forfeit my life, for the furtherance of the ends of justice, and MINGLE MY BLOOD FURTHER WITH THE BLOOD OF MY CHILDREN, and with the blood of millions in this Slave country, whose rights are disregarded by wicked, cruel, and unjust enactments,—I say, LET IT BE DONE.

Let me say one word further: I feel entirely satisfied with the treatment I have received on my trial. Considering all the circumstances, it has been more generous than I expected; but I feel no consciousness of guilt. I have stated from the first what was my *intention,* and what was not. I never had any design against the liberty of any person, nor any disposition to commit treason, or excite Slaves to rebel, or make any general insurrection. I never encouraged any man to do so, but always discouraged any idea of that kind.

Let me say something, also, in regard to the statements made by some of those who were connected with me. I hear that it has been stated by some of them, that I have induced them to join me; but the contrary is true. I do not say this to injure them, but as regarding their weakness. Not one but joined me of his own accord, and the greater part at their own expense. A number of them I never saw and never had a word of conversation with, till the day they came to me, and that was for the purpose I have stated. Now I have done.

John Brown

Printed by C. C. Mead, 91 Washington Street, and for Sale at the LIBERATOR Office, 21 Cornhill, Boston.

Executed on the Scaffold

On December 2, 1859, Brown was taken from the jail to be hanged. A crowd of around 2,000 people had gathered to watch the execution. It was made up of supporters from the North and Southerners who wanted to see him die.

Brown handed a note to his jailer, and now friend, Captain John Avis: "I, John Brown am now quite certain that the crimes of this guilty land: will never be purged away but with Blood. I had, as I now think, vainly flattered myself that without very much bloodshed; it might be done."

Brown mounts the scaffold on December 2, 1859.

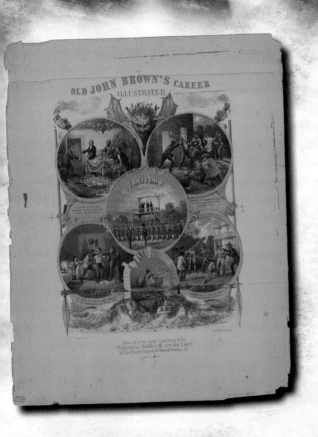

Following Brown's execution, his widow, Mary Ann, took his body home to upstate New York. He was buried there 10 days later.

Brown's Legacy

John Brown was dead but he was not forgotten. The speeches he had made during the trial had caused many Americans to think deeply about the **morality** of slavery. Before the raid on Harpers Ferry, the gulf between the North and South had been growing. Many people still believed, however, that as in the past another compromise would be found and that life in the United States would continue as before. Brown's raid and the public reaction to it made it clear that this was no longer possible.

The political fallout was great. Although every Northern politician condemned the raid, they were less willing to criticize Brown's ideas. In the South, politicians saw Brown as a representative of the new Republican Party. The Republican Party itself was unsure of how best to deal with slavery. The confusion led to Abraham Lincoln being nominated to run for president in the 1860 election. Lincoln was against slavery but did not make the issue part of his election campaign.

FUTURE MEN

AMONG THE OBSERVERS AT JOHN BROWN'S EXECUTION WERE ROBERT E. LEE, THOMAS "STONEWALL" JACKSON, AND JOHN WILKES BOOTH. ALL THREE WOULD PLAY KEY ROLES IN THE CIVIL WAR. LEE AND STONEWALL WERE SENIOR COMMANDERS FOR THE CONFEDERACY. BOOTH WAS A SOUTHERN SYMPATHIZER. HE SHOT PRESIDENT LINCOLN AT FORD'S THEATRE, WASHINGTON, DC, ON APRIL 14, 1865. LINCOLN DIED THE NEXT DAY.

John Wilkes Booth shot Lincoln after the South's defeat in the Civil War.

The 1860 Presidential Election

The Democratic Party was also in a mess. It fielded two candidates in the 1860 election, one from the North and one from the South. With the Democratic vote split, Lincoln won the election despite winning only 40 percent of the popular vote and a million fewer votes than his three opponents.

The election of Lincoln had great consequences. Lincoln had not campaigned on an antislavery ticket, but his election and the Republicans' stance now put the Union on a collision course with the Southern states. Between Lincoln's election and his inauguration as president, seven slaveholding states in the South declared their intention to secede, or leave the Union. As John Brown had predicted in his final note, civil war and huge bloodshed were now unavoidable.

This poster comes from the 1860 presidential election, which Lincoln won. ↓

For President
ABRAM LINCOLN.
For Vice President
HANNIBAL HAMLIN.

TIMELINE

1800   **May 9:** John Brown is born in Torrington, Connecticut.

1805   The Brown family moves to the frontier state of Ohio.

1812   John Brown meets a slave boy on a trip to Fort Detroit and becomes aware of the suffering of slaves.

1820   Brown marries Dianthe Lusk.

1832   **August:** Dianthe Brown dies.

1833   **June 14:** Brown marries his second wife, Mary Ann Day.

1837   Brown loses all his money when an economic crash hits the United States.

c.1845   Brown starts to think about challenging slavery.

1847   Brown meets the abolitionist and former slave Frederick Douglass.

1850   The Fugitive Slave Act is passed. It forces all Americans to help recapture escaped slaves.

1855   **October:** John Brown moves with his family to Kansas, where he forms a militia group to fight the proslavery "Border Ruffians."

1856   **May 21:** Brown and his men witness the burning of Lawrence, Kansas, by proslavers.

       May 22: Antislavery senator Charles Sumner is attacked by a proslavery opponent in the US Senate.

May 24: In the Pottawatomie Massacre, Brown and his men attack the Doyle family home, killing five people. Brown goes on the run from Kansas.

1858 **January 7:** Abolitionists in Massachusetts agree to provide 200 rifles for Brown to begin a slave uprising.

1859 **July 3:** John Brown arrives in Harpers Ferry, Virginia, to plan his raid. A few days later he rents the Kennedy Farmhouse outside the town.

October 16: Brown and his supporters set out for Harpers Ferry.

October 17: Brown's men capture the arsenal. News of the uprising reaches Washington, DC, at about 11 a.m. Virginia militia arrive in Harpers Ferry around midday.

October 18: Brown rejects Robert E. Lee's demand for surrender. Brown is wounded, captured, and interrogated.

October 25: Brown's trial begins in Charles Town.

November 1: Brown is found guilty and sentenced to death. He makes a memorable speech to the court.

December 2: Brown is hanged.

1860 **May:** Abraham Lincoln is nominated as the Republican Party candidate in the presidential election.

November 6: Lincoln is elected president of the United States.

December 20: South Carolina becomes the first state to leave the Union.

1861 **April 12:** Civil war breaks out between the Union and the Confederacy.

GLOSSARY

abolitionists: People who wanted slavery made illegal.

activists: People who campaign for social change.

armories: Places where weapons are made and stored.

arsenal: A collection of weapons and ammunition.

authorities: People who have power to control a region.

compromise: An agreement in which both sides make concessions.

cotton gin: A machine for separating the fibers of cotton.

depression: A long and serious fall in economic activity.

disillusioned: Disappointed by learning that something is not as good as previously believed.

federal: Related to the central US government.

fugitive: Someone who has escaped from captivity.

hostage: A person who is captured and held to make sure that certain conditions or demands are fulfilled.

institution: An established practice or way of behaving.

insurgents: People who are taking part in a revolt.

insurrection: A violent uprising against authority or a government.

interrogation: An examination in which someone is questioned over a long period.

labor intensive: Describes a task that requires many workers.

lynched: Executed for an alleged crime without a legal trial.

massacre: A brutal killing of many people.

militia: A military force formed by civilians.

morality: The values that decide whether behavior is right or wrong.

musket: A long-barreled gun.

sacrifice: Something that is given up in order to achieve a purpose.

skirmishes: Small-scale fights.

slavery: The owning of people as possessions.

speculation: Trying to make money through risky investments.

telegraph: A system for sending messages over electrical wires.

terrorize: To influence someone's behavior by making them afraid.

truce: A temporary halt in fighting.

FURTHER INFORMATION

Books

Crompton, Samuel Willard.
The Raid on Harpers Ferry: John Brown's Rebellion. Milestones in American History. New York: Chelsea House Publications, 2010.

Schraff, Anne E.
John Brown: We Came to Free the Slaves. Americans: The Spirit of a Nation. Berkeley Heights, NJ: Enslow Publishers, 2010.

Stefoff, Rebecca.
John Brown and Armed Resistance to Slavery. Primary Sources of the Abolitionist Movement. New York: Cavendish Square Publishing, 2015.

Yomtov, Nel.
John Brown: Defending the Innocent or Plotting Terror? Perspectives on History. North Mankato, MN: Capstone Press, 2013.

Websites

http://www.ducksters.com/history/civil_war/john_brown_and_the_harpers_ferry_raid.php
A Ducksters.com page about John Brown with a biography and details about the raid on Harpers Ferry.

http://www.eyewitnesstohistory.com/johnbrown.htm
An eyewitness account of the fighting at Harpers Ferry written by Robert E. Lee.

http://www.history.com/topics/john-brown
A biography of John Brown from History.com with links to a number of videos.

http://www.american-historama.org/1850-1860-secession-era/john-brown-biography.htm
A timeline and list of fun facts about John Brown's life and the raid on Harpers Ferry.

Publisher's note to educators and parents: Our editors have carefully reviewed these websites to ensure that they are suitable for students. Many websites change frequently, however, and we cannot guarantee that a site's future contents will continue to meet our high standards of quality and educational value. Be advised that students should be closely supervised whenever they access the Internet.

INDEX